Tarporley & Beeston Country

R.M.BEVAN

First published in 2006
by C.C.Publishing
(Chester)

First reprint
ISBN
0 949001 32 5

*C.C. PUBLISHING, MARTINS LANE, HARGRAVE, CHESTER, CH3 7RX
TEL: 01829 741651. EMAIL: editor@cc-publishing.co.uk
WEBSITE: http://www.cc-publishing.co.uk*

*Front cover illustration: Oulton Hall, from a print in the
possession of Capt. Gordon Fergusson.*

INTRODUCTION

There are books galore about Cheshire, most with little more than a passing reference to the surrounds of Tarporley and Beeston. Only Beeston Castle, that ancient sentinel of the Cheshire Plain, is guaranteed to fleetingly capture a writer's interest and perhaps then only as a convenient interlude twixt Chester and Nantwich. The very ruralness of the district dictates this has always been so and it leaves us with disjointed snippets of information in a plethora of publications, from county tomes to village histories, the latter admirably covering some of the individual parochial confines of Tarporley, Eaton, Little Budworth, Alpraham, Tilstone Fearnall, Tiverton, Bunbury and Peckforton. This book, *Tarporley & Beeston Country*, based upon a personal collection of nostalgic photographs, is an overview of the district, a bringing together of the pieces with the addition of previously unpublished material, into a broader, local picture depicting the timelessness of this unique part of Cheshire with its castles and its discernible thread of history stretching into English antiquity. Along the way I have been particularly indebted to Allan Earl, Ann Billington, Alan Sheen and Tom Wright who possess an immeasurable wealth of local knowledge. They have also provided additional illustrations, as have John Mears, Chris Pitt, Roy Ramsbottom, Brian Pennington, Gordon Fergusson and Gary P. Calveley. Gordon Fergusson's *The Green Collars* and Roy Ramsbottom's *Marching As To War*, both outstanding works, have been unparalleled sources of reference.

R.M.BEVAN

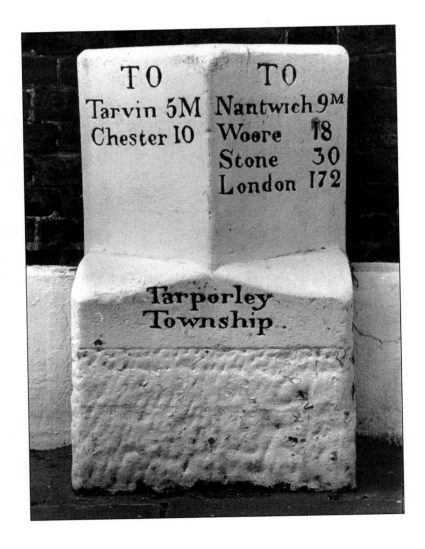

The Domesday Book records a settlement at "Torpelei" and as early as 1287 Tarporley had its own Mayor. In medieval times it was granted the right to stage a market and a three-day fair. The top photograph shows the Swan Hotel, Tarporley's best known landmark. The bottom view of the High Street is probably taken from the Manor House.

T.A.Coward, in *Picturesque Cheshire* (1904), noted of Tarporley: "It is just far enough from the railway to keep it remote from the noise and bustle of the great North West line, but near enough to be in touch with the outer world. The houses that line the street are old-fashioned but not decayed, the few shops have an air of respectable prosperity without appearing too much up-to-date.".

The noted author, Beatrice Tunstall, writing half a century ago, considered the village of Bunbury "a real bit of old Cheshire fundamentally unchanged for five hundred years...".

Beeston Castle & Tarporley Station in about 1910. The cattle and livestock trade associated with Beeston Market ensured this was one of the busiest railway stations on the Chester-Crewe line.

The coming together of canal and railway at Beeston. This view, looking up the hill towards Tiverton, has changed little over the past century.

Remains of a Bronze Age settlement dating from around 800BC have been found on Beeston Crag. Beeston Castle has dominated the local landscape since the 13th century.

Two idyllic rural scenes from Cotebrook, early 20th century, when farming was the mainstay of the local economy. The lower photograph shows St John's Church, Cotebrook.

Two photographs of the Headless Woman public house, Duddon. The top view dates from the 1920s and shows Duddon Post Office (now demolished) before the A51 was widened between Tarporley and Tarvin. The bottom photograph is considerably earlier.

Time to stand and stare in old Eaton village.

A sense of timelessness in Little Budworth eighty years ago. For many centuries the manor and village of Budworth-le-Frith was held by the Grosvenors and the Talbots, Earls of Shrewsbury.

EARLY HISTORY

Bunbury Church, dedicated to St Boniface, is said to be one of the finest examples of a medieval church anywhere in England.

The foundations of St Helen's Church, Tarporley, a Victorian gothic restoration, date from the 14th century. There were Saxon and Norman settlements at both Bunbury and Tarporley.

Ranulph de Blundeville, 6th Earl of Chester, fired by the architectural wonders he had seen in the Holy Lands, in 1220 set about building a castle stronghold on Beeston Crag with its commanding views of eight counties ..."that famous and far-seen castle" wrote William Webb in 1656.

The first line of works were apparently inspired by the walls of old Constantinople and the rounded drum towers from the early Crusader castles. So fearsome were the fortifications that King Henry III commandeered Beeston as an official Royal Castle and so it remained until the reign of Elizabeth I.

Legend has it that shortly before his death King Richard II, en route to Ireland, stored his vast personal treasure here. "200,000 marks in gold coin and other objects" still remain hidden in the castle's 360-feet deep well. Despite strenuous efforts and the advent of modern technology, not a single coin from the hoard has ever been unearthed.

Beeston Castle is now a major tourist attraction run by English Heritage. The photograph, right, shows visitors circa 1910.

Delamere Forest extends to little more than 2,400 acres in the 21st century. In medieval times it covered an area of sixty square miles and encompassed fifty townships, from the River Gowy to the River Weaver, from Frodsham in the west, to the outskirts of Nantwich in the east. This was the twin forest of Mara and Mondrem, "Forest de la Mare" to the Normans. At the approximate centre, near to "Peytefinsty", the ancient forest track that historians say was the dividing boundary between Mara and Mondrem, was Tarporley and, just outside the forest confines, the Saxon settlement of Bunbury. The modern A49 is generally believed to follow the approximate route of "Peytefinsty", though it is more likely to have been to the east, as traced by a network of back roads, footpaths and green lanes that suggest it ran a more obvious course from Tarporley Church, via Eaton Cross, Little Budworth Church, Sandiway and Gorstage, to the church and River Weaver crossing at Weaverham.

The Normans built a church at Bunbury, dedicated to St Boniface, and this was replaced with today's magnificent cathedral-like structure during the 14th century, at the expense of Sir Hugh Calveley. A giant of a man, reputedly 7ft tall, Sir Hugh was born in Calveley in 1315 and served with distinction in France under the Black Prince and later became Governor of the Channel Isles. This at least is the popular myth, though the truth is Sir Hugh was no saint, far from it. During his campaigns, and when deputy governor of Calais, he lit

The site of a medieval preaching cross at Eaton, reputed to have been removed to Tarporley in Puritan times. Evidence of Roman occupation has been discovered at Eaton.

the morning sky with the flames of twenty-six burning ships in Boulogne harbour while his men sacked the town. Next year he spoiled St Malo and Etaples and raged terrible attacks along the coast of Britanny. T.A. Coward in *Picturesque Cheshire* says of him: "Smoking byres and shrieking women and the gruesome sights of war were bread and cheese to Sir Hugh".

Following a close shave with death during a shipwreck, Sir Hugh returned to Cheshire posing as a "good man" and gave, from his ill-gotten gains, a hospital to Rome and also founded the church at Bunbury. His magnificent effigy, his wealth and his generosity have succeeded in air-brushing the worst of his deeds from history. In 1387 St Boniface, Bunbury, was elevated to a collegiate church, with a master and six chaplains. It passed to the Crown in 1547.

The Tarporley and Bunbury district is altogether steeped in Delamere Forest history, rooted as deep as the ancient English oak that once clothed great swathes of the surrounding countryside, and to this day is still associated with the customs, privileges and laws that have governed these parts for a thousand years.

CHURCH OF ST. BONIFACE, BUNBURY

Sir Hugh Calveley's effigy in Bunbury Church. Also here is the tomb of Sir George Beeston who fought for Queen Elizabeth in numerous battles, including the Armada. He was knighted at the age of eighty-nine.

DONE OF UTKINTON, FLAXYARDS AND DUDDON
ARMS Azure, two barrs Argent, overall, on a bend Gules, three arrows Argent.
CREST 1st, on a wreath eight Arrows in saltire, 4 and 4, points downwards, Or, feathered Sable, banded Gules; 2nd, on a wreath, a Buck's Head erased proper, attired Or.
*e as described in Ormerod's 'History of Cheshire'.

The Done coat of arms.

"Forest de la Mare" was a Royal forest, jealously guarded through harsh and cruel laws introduced by William the Conqueror to ensure that all hunting and game preservation remained vested in the Crown. Miscreants, normally the peasantry, were dealt with severely and anyone caught in the act of poaching faced short shrift on the end of a rope.

The Crown's representative in the forest and holding almost exclusive powers over life and death was the hereditary Master Forester and Chief Bowbearer, the first of whom was Ralph (Ranulph) de Kingsley who was granted the title in 1123 by the 3rd Earl of Chester. The symbol of his authority was a black horn that came to be known as the "Delamere Horn".

Through marriage and inheritance, the office of Master Forester passed to Henry Done, of Utkinton, and remained in the Done family for over four-hun-

Utkinton Hall, now a rambling farmhouse, dates from the Elizabethan period but is only a quarter of its original size. It was the seat of the Master Forester Dones and once contained a chapel and a dungeon. It was plundered of its plate and jewels by the Royalists in 1644 and the stained glass and a staircase were removed to Tarporley Rectory in the 18th century. The glass then went to Vale Royal (Whitegate) and is now in the Burrell Collection, Glasgow. This view dates from the early 20th century and shows many of the windows blocked. The frontage to the road and the once magnificent tall brick gate-piers were built around 1700 for Sir John Crewe.

The timber-framed, now rendered, Manor House on Tarporley High Street was built in 1585/86 by Ralph Done, the Master Forester of Delamere. The initials RD with the Utkinton coat of arms are recorded on one of the gable ends.

dred years. Sir John Done (1577-1629), the 19th Master Forester, was actually knighted at Utkinton Hall, in 1617, by King James I following a day's hunting in the forest. "Arise Sir John – a gentleman very complete in many excellencies of nature, wit and ingenuity."

The last of the true Dones associated with the Master Forestership was Mary Done who married into the influential Crewe family. Her son, Sir John Crewe, became the 23rd Master Forester. Through the female line the title and estates then passed into the Arden family whose best known son was Richard Pepper Arden, Chief Justice of the Court of Common Pleas, who, in 1801, became Baron Alvanley, of Alvanley. The female line was obviously stronger in the genes of the Master Foresters and thus the title descended through marriage to

Sir John Done, knighted by King James at Utkinton.

George Baillie-Hamilton (Lord Binning) the 11th Earl of Haddington, in whose family the Delamere Horn was carried until 1959. The ancient title of Master Forester is now vested in the 36th holder, Karen Cowan, a descendant, through the O'Brien family, of the Baillie-Hamiltons.

Monuments in Tarporley Church, the last remnants of Utkinton Hall, the former moated Flaxyards Hall, once mighty Arderne Hall and the ever enigmatic Tarporley Manor House are part of an indelible and rich local heritage left in these parts by centuries of successive Master Foresters.

Still as pretty as a picture. Utkinton... the power base of the Dones of Delamere Forest.

It was Lord Haddington who, in 1867, built Arderne Hall on an elevated position on the outskirts of Tarporley village, on the site of Eaton Banks House, the one-time home of General Richard Egerton who had distinguished himself at the Battle of Waterloo.

In its heyday, at the turn of the 20th century, the Arderne Hall estate comprised over 4,200 acres and was the major employer in the Tarporley area. The hall was demolished in 1959 following the death of Lady Grisell Baillie-Hamilton and a large modern house was erected in its place by the O'Brien family.

Richard Pepper Arden, Baron Alvanley.

Arderne Hall, the home of Lord Haddington and the Baillie-Hamilton family, survived for less than a century. It was designed in the popular mid-Victorian gothic style. Below is the grand entrance hall.

Two well known local hostelries linked with the families of Master Foresters of Delamere. The top photograph shows the Alvanley Arms, Cotebrook, a former coaching inn once owned by Lord Haddington. The cottage to the left was demolished circa 1960. Below is the Crewe Arms (now The Yewtree), at Bunbury, originally part of the Earl of Crewe's Spurstow estates.

CIVIL WAR

August 22nd, 1642 came to be a watershed in English history for upon this date King Charles I raised the Royal Standard at Nottingham and so began the Civil War between Royalists and Parliamentarians. In the coming years the bloody struggle enveloped the nation and nowhere was it more acutely experienced than in the countryside around Tarporley, midway between the strategically important towns of Nantwich and Chester, the latter with its sea-port to Ireland.

Beeston Castle, for so long neglected and ruinous, was at the heart of the Cheshire conflict. At its foot ran the old Roman road to Whitchurch (the present A49); two miles away was the London-Chester road (the present A51); three miles to the south was the road from the Midlands, through Nantwich and over the Dee at Farndon, to Wrexham and North Wales; five miles to the north was the road from Chester to Manchester. The historian R.N.Dore wrote in his account, *Beeston Castle in the Great Civil War 1643-46*: "Perched on its great crag, a garrison could spy out the movement of enemy troops and provisions along any of these roads, and either attack them or send on information about them to headquarters."

Beeston was, indeed, a prize and, having taken the town of Nantwich, Sir William Brereton, the commander of the Parliamentarian forces in Cheshire, wasted little time in seizing the castle with a force of 300 troops. On the following day, in February 1643, some of the men sallied forth to assist their comrades on Rhudall Heath, Tilstone Heath and Tiverton Town Field. The following excellent description appears in *The Story of Cheshire*:

"A portion of the Nantwich garrison marched out and reduced Beeston Castle. This was a serious disaster for the King's party since the stronghold commanded the road to Chester. Another force set out from Nantwich for Tarporley, to attend a muster there, but found their way blocked at Tilstone Heath by the Chester Royalists who had with them two large guns. There appears to have been a good deal of shooting but, we are told, little or no hurt was done. Hearing the firing, the party, which had captured the castle, sallied out and another skirmish took place on Tiverton Common. In this both sides suffered. The officers who fell, friend and foe, were buried together at Tarporley."

The strategic position of Lower Huxley Hall proved critical in the struggle for Beeston Castle.

The castle remained under Brereton's men until it was suddenly seized during an audacious raid by a handful of Royalist firelocks led by Captain Thomas Sandford. The castle commander, Captain Thomas Steele, was forced to surrender with sixty men and though allowed to leave with his "colours flying", the Parliamentary War Council, at Nantwich, decided that he was a traitor and he was executed in Tinker's Croft, at the east end of Nantwich Parish Church.

Burton Hall, though now rather weather-worn, has stood strong and dignified for over four hundred years. During the Civil War it was home to the Royalist family of Werden, one of whom from here plotted the looting of Utkinton Hall which was held by the Parliamentarian Sir John Crewe.

Sir William Brereton was not to be denied and as the fortunes of war tilted one way and then the other, he finally got his revenge by recapturing Beeston in 1645 at a time when the Royalists were already reeling from defeat at the Chester Battle of Rowton Moor. As one 17th century writer put it: "Theire was neither meate, Ale nor Beere found in the Castle, save onelie a peece of Turkey pye, Twoe Bisketts, a lyve Peacock and a Peahen. Theye had eaten theire cats and hade not provision for that night."

Just how difficult life must have been for the folks around these parts is gleaned from the following brief references: November 16, 1644: Brereton, hearing that the castle's Royalist garrison are short of supplies, begins intense siege.

December 7, 1644: Forty or fifty Royalists burst out of the castle and catch a group of twenty-six Parliamentary soldiers at dinner, all of whom are killed, except two who are taken back into the castle as prisoners.

March 17, 1645: Prince Rupert and Prince Maurice relieve the castle and plunder almost all of Bunbury parish.

June 9, 1645: Eaton and Rushton - three cavalry troops and six infantry companies of Royalists from Chester attack Captain Glegg's troop in their quarters. He is rescued by forces from Tarvin who pursue the Royalists to the borders of Delamere Forest, killing ten and capturing over two-hundred for the loss of three Parliamentarians.

Many large houses in the district were garrisoned, or looted by one side or the other. Lower Huxley Hall, Tattenhall Hall, Oulton Hall, Utkinton Hall, Hockenhull Hall, Duddon Hall and Burton Hall were amongst the survivors listed on the roll of dishonour. Not so fortunate were Tilstone Hall, at Tilstone Fearnall, the home of Sir Richard Wilbraham, which was all but destroyed and Beeston Hall, burned to the ground by Prince Rupert's Royalists in 1645.

Within two months of the surrender of Beeston Castle, warrants were sent

This gruesome reminder of the Civil War once stood in the gardens of the Headless Woman public house, Duddon. It supposedly depicted the story of a Royalist serving wench who refused to reveal to Parliamentarian troops the whereabouts of the family plate at nearby Hockenhull Hall. She kept her mouth shut and lost her head! The figure itself was apparently acquired to embellish the legend in the 1930s by a former seafaring landlord from the stern of a ship.

Typical Cheshire. Duddon Hall was a key location between Beeston Castle and Chester. The Battle of Tarvin, August 1644, was one of the bloodiest and saw the Royalist forces routed.

out to the constables of Tarporley, Bunbury, Wrenbury and Acton to organise the destruction of the Beeston defences and by the following summer of 1646 the deed was accomplished, with only the gatehouse and parts of some of the towers left standing.

The vicar of Tarporley at this time was Nathaniel Lancaster, a strong Puritan who became the official chaplain to the Parliamentarian army as it besieged Chester. Afterwards, and published by order of Parliament, he wrote an account of the fighting, a copy of which is retained in the British Museum.

Of greater local significance, though perhaps an even lesser known fact, is that the village of Bunbury is directly connected to the execution of King Charles I. The story goes that in 1576 Thomas Aldersey, a haberdasher of London, and a member of the influential Aldersey family, of Spurstow, founded Aldersey Grammar School, in Bunbury. It was a fee-paying establishment, held in the highest regard, and the sons of many well-heeled families from throughout the region were educated here. One scholar, the son of a landowner, was John Bradshaw, born in Stockport in 1602, who went on to train for a career in the legal profession. In 1647 he was appointed Chief Justice of Cheshire and North Wales and, as Parliament's Lord President, was charged with trying King Charles in 1649. History tells us it was President Bradshaw who, "damned to everlasting fame", passed the death sentence on "Charles Stuart Tyrant".

The official entry of Bradshaw's birth in Stockport, reads: "December 1602. John the sonne of Henry Bradshaw (etc.) baptised the tenth." Someone in later years added a single, bitter word.... "traitor"! John Bradshaw died in 1659. After

Oulton Hall, the home at Little Budworth of the Egertons and later the Grey-Egertons, was an important "moated" outpost in the Civil War siege of Chester. A letter survives in the Egerton papers from King Charles I personally requesting a loan from the family of £2,000, for the "maintenance of our army which we are compelled to raise for the defence of our person, the Protestant religion, and the laws of the land". The King did not survive but Oulton Hall did and seventy years later, in the early part of the 18th century, John Egerton commissioned a new hall, seen in this print, dated 1733. He spent the staggering sum of £42,000 on the project, allegedly working to designs prepared by Sir John Vanbrugh, the architect of Blenheim Palace and Castle Howard, in Yorkshire. One cannot confirm this, but the design of Oulton Hall (greatly altered in the 19th century) bears remarkable similarities with Castle Howard. And Vanbrugh, of course, did have early local connections; he lived with his parents in Chester and for some years attended King's School. (Reproduced by permission of the Cheshire Record Office.)

John Bradshaw.

the Restoration a special court was appointed and in October 1660 those Regicides who were still alive and living in Britain were brought to trial. Ten were found guilty and were sentenced to be hung, drawn and quartered. Bradshaw, Oliver Cromwell, Henry Ireton and Thomas Pride were all posthumously tried for high treason. They were found guilty and in January 1661 their corpses were exhumed and hung in chains at Tyburn.

A stained glass window in the vestry of Bunbury Church depicts an Elizabethan lady who is believed to have been Bradshaw's mother.

Bunbury's Aldersey School listed amongst its more celebrated scholars Admiral David Beatty of First World War "Battle of Jutland" fame. He was born in 1871, at Stapeley, near Nantwich, and as a boy moved to live near to Tarporley with his parents who devoted themselves to hunting and training horses.

Beeston Castle (from Tattenhall Lanes.)

Anstons New So

Many skirmishes in the struggle for Beeston Castle occurred in the labyrinth of lanes as every ditch and hollow was contested by Roundhead and Cavalier.

HUNTING COUNTRY

The swallow flies fast, but remember
The swallow with summer is gone;
What bird is there left in November
To rival the Tarporley Swan?

Hunting in these parts requires little introduction. Suffice to say that the district has been at the centre of the sport since the Normans and Tarporley itself boasts Britain's oldest Hunt Club which, despite the politically incorrectness of modern times, will shortly celebrate the 250th anniversary of its founding, in 1762.

Originally a small, exclusive club of nine privileged sporting parsons and gentlemen sons of the gentry, it was established to advance a shared passion for hare hunting. Some of the early members had their own packs of hounds, others kept harriers for hunting. The founders, all in their twenties, were the Rev. Obadiah Lane, of Longton, Staffordshire, the first President; John Crewe, the son of the

When a Swan takes to singing they say she will die; But our Tarporley Swan proves that legend a lie; For a hundred years past she has swung at this door; May she swing there and sing there a thousand years more!
- R.E.Egerton-Warburton, 1862.

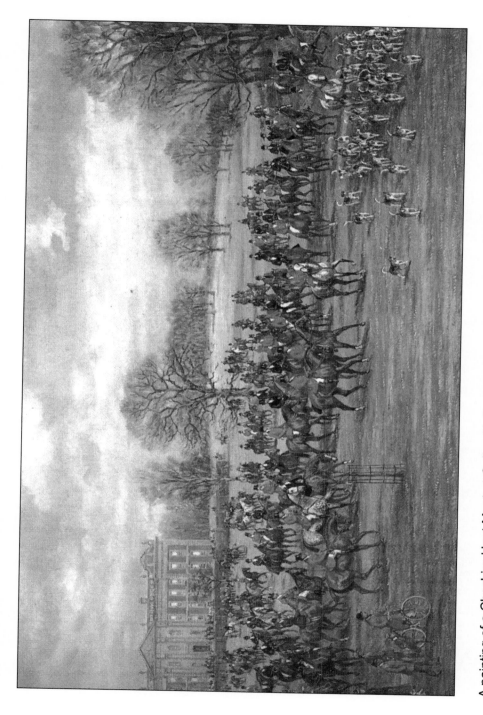

A painting of a Cheshire Hunt Meet at Oulton Hall apparently during the years when Fred Champion was Huntsman, 1903-1911. He was great uncle to the legendary Bob Champion, Grand National victor on Aldaniti, in 1981.

Rev. Dr Joseph Crewe, Rector of Astbury; The Hon Booth Grey, of Wincham; Sir Henry Mainwaring, 4th and last Baronet of Over Peover; George and Roger Wilbraham, sons of Roger Wilbraham, of Townsend, Nantwich; The Rev. Edward Emily who came from Woking, Surrey; Richard Walthall, of Wistaston, Crewe; Robert Salisbury Cotton, of Combermere Abbey.

Over the years membership rose gradually and in 1806 reached forty, where it has remained ever since. Membership, of what is now essentially a Dining Club, is by invitation only and, according to the names and crests on the Presidential boards, is often a family affair, passing from father to son. The names stand out like cameos in the aristocratic and military history of Cheshire. For instance, in 1910, membership included: Lord Barrymore, Earl of Enniskillen, Earl of Haddington, Baron Von Schroder, Lord Arthur Grosvenor, Sir Humphrey De Trafford, Sir L.Delves Broughton, Sir Philip Grey-Egerton, Sir Gilbert Greenall, Earl of Shrewsbury, Earl of Crewe, Duke of Westminster, Lord Tollemache, Marquess of Cholmondeley.

Fines can still be imposed for all manner of rule transgressions. In the early days any member on the occasion of marriage was to present each of his fellow members with a pair of well-stitched buckskin breeches, which was later modified to a presentation of twenty sovereigns to the club, a rule which still exists.

Incorrectness of dress is something members have always been particular

Tarporley... a rare hunting village.

Willington Hall, Willington. Now a celebrated local hotel & restaurant, this fine house was built in 1829, for Colonel William Tomkinson, of Nantwich, a retired cavalry officer from the Peninsular and Waterloo campaigns. The Colonel's son, James Tomkinson, was a leading member of the Tarporley Hunt Club who became MP for Crewe. He was a dare-devil rider in the hunting field and died when he was seventy, from a fall whilst riding in the House of Commons Point-to-Point in 1910.

about. The original uniform was a blue frock coat with scarlet velvet cape, but since 1770 has remained more or less unchanged... scarlet coat with green collar, green breeches and waistcoat and green silk stockings. This was an attire not agreeable to everyone and in 1811, when commissioned to produce a portait of Sir Peter Warburton, a past President, the distinguished artist Sir William Beechey complained that "he might as well paint a parrot!".

The green collars have long been synonymous with members of the Tarporley Hunt Club and, in 1993, provided a fitting title, *The Green Collars*, to Gordon Fergusson's quite superb book "... to put on record the annals of the oldest continuously surviving hunt club in England".

The centenary of the club was celebrated in 1862 with a Ball at the Old Royal

Hotel, Chester and one of the guests of honour was William Ewart Gladstone, of Hawarden, who at the time was Chancellor of the Exchequer. The bi-centenary Ball took place at Arley Hall, home of the then President, Lord Ashbrook.

The Swan Hotel has always been the headquarters of the Tarporley Hunt Club whose badge depicts a white swan encircled by the motto "Quaesitum Meritis". Rowland Egerton Warburton, Tarporley Hunt Club's own celebrated rhyme-master, wrote:

> A club of good fellows, we meet once a year,
> When the leaves of the Forest are yellow and sear;
> By the motto that shines on each glass it is shown
> We pledge in our cups the deserving alone;
> Our glass a quaesitum ourselves Cheshire men;
> May we fill it and drink it again and again.

The Meet at Calveley Hall, an elegant residence associated for centuries with hunting and the Tarporley Hunt Club through the Tollemache family, the Grosvenors and the Midwoods. This was the second Calveley Hall and dated from the 18th century. It was demolished during the 1950s. Squire Davenport, of the earlier hall, is reputed to have entertained John Wesley at Calveley Hall, in 1749. (Photograph reproduced by permission of Gary P Calveley.)

Cholmondeley Castle: A half-timbered manor house, complete with moat and draw-bridge, was demolished to make way for the 1st Marquess of Cholmondeley's stately pile, built 1800-1804. The Cholmondeleys hold the hereditary title of Lord Great Chamberlain of England.

Peckforton has been prominent in local hunting circles since it was built as a mock medieval castle in 1850/51. It was designed by Anthony Salvin for John Tollemache who, in 1876, became 1st Baron Tollemache of Helmingham. The principal family seat of the Tollemaches was in Helmingham, Suffolk and through the female line they also held the Earldom of Dysart. Lord Tollemache spent a fortune creating Peckforton Castle. The building materials were from his 26,000-acre Cheshire estates upon which he is said to have spent £280,000, modernising and refurbishing the farmsteads and cottages. Lord Tollemache served as MP for South Cheshire and, by two marriages, fathered twenty-four sons and one daughter. He died in 1890.

The background to this extraordinary piece of Cheshire whimsy, in a cottage garden in Peckforton village, has provoked many a discussion. All that is known definitely is that it was carved out of Peckforton sandstone by local master stonemason John Watson; that it originally stood in his own garden and was intended as a beehive, though never used as such. The consensus is that Watson personally chose an "Elephant & Castle" because it featured in the arms of the Corbets who owned Peckforton up to about 1626. In fact, the elaborate sculpture was commissioned by Edwin Corbet, once of Darnhall Hall but in the 1850s residing at Tilstone Lodge. Watson was taking commissions at this time as evidenced by two pairs of stone lions which he also carved and which now adorn houses in Spurstow and Tattenhall. So why did Edwin Corbet not collect the finished work? Because, as a white marble tablet in Tilstone Fearnall Parish Church notes, he died in 1858, precisely at the time Watson was completing the work. Included on the memorial "Sacred to the memory of Edwin Corbet" is the family crest, an Elephant & Castle.

Tilstone Lodge, Tilstone Fearnall. Originally a small farmhouse, greatly altered and enlarged by Rear Admiral Halliday and his wife Lady Louisa Tollemache, the parents of the 1st Baron Tollemache and founders of Tilstone Fearnall Parish Church. After Edwin Corbet's death it was occupied by Major Cyril Dewhurst. The Corbet and Dewhurst families are entwined in the annals of the Tarporley Hunt Club. Another "green collar" and later resident, from 1936, was Sir Harold Bibby, Chairman of the Bibby Shipping Line.

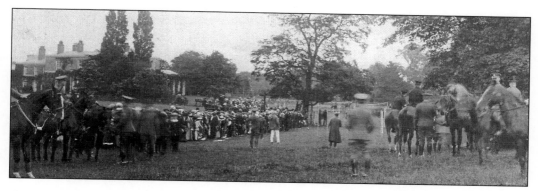

One of the popular local events of the Edwardian period was Tilstone Lodge's Annual Garden Party, seen here in all its splendour, around 1908.

Gardenhurst, Tiverton. Built in 1886 as a hunting residence for James Gordon Houghton. After the Second World War it was converted into Hampton House School for Boys, an establishment that survived until 1963. A number of dwellings and the Deeside Ramblers' sporting facilities now occupy most of the original four-acre site.

Oulton Hall underwent major changes in the 19th century. It evolved into the magnificent, palatial home of the Grey-Egertons which came to be one of the great centres of Cheshire hunting and shooting. The entertainment was lavish in the beautiful Baroque mansion surrounded by its 315 acres of walled parkland, grazed by an enormous deer herd.

Haughton Hall, Bunbury, held by the Haughton family until about 1740. In 1889, with the Manor of Haughton, it was acquired by Ralph Brocklebank, of the Brocklebank Shipping Line. His principal heir, Sir Aubrey Brocklebank, built Nunsmere Hall, Oakmere, and when the Brocklebank Line merged with Cunard, Sir Aubrey took on the responsibility of planning a prestigious new liner. At Nunsmere Hall he mused over thousands of plans and experiments before recommending a vast ship, 1,000 ft. overall length and 81,000 gross tonnage. It came to be the Queen Mary, launched in 1934.

Nunsmere, Oakmere where Sir Aubrey Brocklebank mused over the plans and experiments for the mighty Queen Mary.

Tirley Gath, Utkinton. Designed by C.E.Mallows and built 1906-12, Tirley Garth was for many decades during the 20th century a spiritual home and world centre for the Moral Rermament movement.

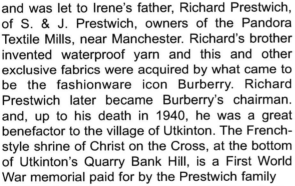

Behind MRA at Tirley Garth (originally called Tirley Court) was the remarkable Miss Irene Prestwich (below right) who as a young woman had moved into the property with her parents and her sister Lois. Tirley Garth was owned by the Northwich chemical firm of Brunner Mond and was let to Irene's father, Richard Prestwich, of S. & J. Prestwich, owners of the Pandora Textile Mills, near Manchester. Richard's brother invented waterproof yarn and this and other exclusive fabrics were acquired by what came to be the fashionware icon Burberry. Richard Prestwich later became Burberry's chairman. and, up to his death in 1940, he was a great benefactor to the village of Utkinton. The French-style shrine of Christ on the Cross, at the bottom of Utkinton's Quarry Bank Hill, is a First World War memorial paid for by the Prestwich family

Whilst enjoying the isolation of Tirley Garth, Richard's daughters missed the intellectual stimulation of Manchester and consequently decided to formally join their local church. This led to Irene attending a conference organised by the Oxford Group which became the Moral Rearmament Movement, an evangelical interpretation of Christianity, committed to raising the moral tone of all aspects of 20th century society. To Irene it was God's work and she set her heart to support MRA and its inspirational leader, Frank Buchman. Following the death of her parents and the ending of the Second World War she purchased Tirley Garth outright and through a trust generously gifted it to MRA. As she said before her death in 1970 she had a vision for Tirley Garth. "In my mind's eye I saw throngs of people coming with their problems and going out with God."

Tirley Garth has returned to private ownership and is now occupied by the television producer Phil Redmond.

I.P.P., 1893

Mr. and Mrs. R. H. Prestwich, my father and mother, in the dining room of Tirley Garth, 1934

Family life at Tirley Garth, from Irene Prestwich's own book.

Tilstone House, Tilstone Fearnall. Like many large properties in the area it was built in the 19th century as a hunting lodge, here for a member of the Greenall brewing family. When it came up for auction in 1955 it was listed as a mansion, with grounds and stabling, two cottages, a lodge and two acres of market garden. It was withdrawn at £7,750.

Top left: One of the district's oldest surviving dwellings, Parkwall Cottage, in the shadow of Oulton Park. Top right: Stapleford Hall in the 1890s, probably at the time when it was occupied by the Lea family. Middle: Quaint old Fishers Green, near Tarporley. Left: Whitehall, Little Budworth, a mansion originally built for the Earl of Shrewsbury.

The third of Tarporley & Beeston Country's castles is Bolesworth, built in the mid-18th century for James Tilson. Later it was owned by John Crewe and, in 1805, acquired by Thomas Tarleton, of Aigburth Hall, Liverpool. Three of his sons were in partnership in one of Britain's leading slave trade companies and Tarleton personally owned

estates and cotton plantations in the West Indies. He also had negro slaves at Bolesworth Castle, and Harthill Church intriguingly records, in 1807, the birth of a base (illegitimate) child to "William, a Negro, late servant at Bolesworth Castle and Ann Wilson of Harthill, servant". This must have been quite a local scandal as well as a personal tragedy, the inference being that the father, the"late servant", had been sold and shipped away! When Tarleton died in 1820, thirteen years before the Abolition of Slavery, he bequeathed his slaves, buildings, stores, cotton etc, in Dominica and Grenada, to his son-in-law, the Rev William Wickham Drake of Malpas. The next owner of Bolesworth was George Walmseley who rebuilt the castle circa 1829. Later it passed, via Thomas Crallan, to Robert Barbour, a Scottish-born, Manchester shipping magnate. The last major alterations and extensions were designed by Clough Williams-Ellis of Portmeirion fame. Robert Barbour's family continues to own the Bolesworth estate.

The Hunt meets at the Fox & Barrel, Cotebrook.

BUNBURY, BEESTON & TIVERTON

Photographers were obviously an attraction in themselves when these two views of picturesque Bunbury were taken, one in front of the old post office and the other showing Brantwood, a brick cottage where the one-man village lock-up was sited.

Public Hall & Post Office

Bunbury Village Hall, a Red Cross hospital during the First World War. The top view shows the post office and the hall in the 1930s.

Left: The Nags Head, Bunbury, is far older than it appears. It is recorded as being a beerhouse as early as 1717.

Higher Bunbury. The former village post office and Church Row cottages demolished on the night of November 28, 1940 when a landmine wrought havoc on Bunbury Church.

The Dysart Arms, previously established in a nearby cottage, takes its name from the Tollemache family of Peckforton, Earls of Dysart.

Bunbury School, founded as a grammar school in 1594 by village benefactor Thomas Aldersey, remains under the unique patronage of the Worshipful Company of Haberdashers, a City of London Livery Company. Another village to have connections with the City of London is Hargrave. Thomas Moulson, the son of a Hargrave family, became a Freeman of the Worshipful Company of Grocers in 1601 and Lord Mayor of London in 1634. He lived in a large house on the site of what is now the Bank of England. Having found

fame and fortune he set up a trust and built a combined school and chapel, St Peter's Church, Hargrave. Though the school closed in 1954, the Sir Thomas Moulson Trust continues to support the church and the accompanying church hall and playing field.

The Image House, on the A49, is said to have been erected in a night, between sunset and sunrise, a "squatter's cottage". The builder was reputedly a local poacher sentenced to transportation. Upon his return, he built the cottage and adorned the exterior with rough likenesses of the gamekeepers, constables and justices who had sentenced him. It is now a listed building though most of the images have gone. Beatrice Tunstall immortalised the story in her book "The Shiny Night".

The village and name of Bunbury is etched into British sporting history and the blue riband of horse racing, the Epsom Derby. The instigators of this legendary race in 1780 were the Earl of Derby and Sir Charles Bunbury (right) who, unable to agree on a name, tossed a coin and the Derby, rather than the Bunbury, it became.

Ironically the first ever Derby was won by Sir Charles's horse Diomed. Sir Charles (1740-1821), founder and perpetual president of the Jockey Club for upwards of forty years, was a direct descendant of the Norman house of St Pierre who came to England with the Conqueror and was granted the manor and lands of Bunbury. The Baron de Pierre's eldest son, Henry, was thus titled Henry de Bunbury.

A later Henry, the seventh in descent from St Pierre, acquired by marriage the lordship of Stanney and following the Coronation of King James I, in 1603, was knighted Sir Henry Bunbury. Sir Charles, the racing doyen, was the 6th Baronet. Also from this branch of the Bunbury family came Lieutenant H.W. St Pierre Bunbury after whom the city of Bunbury, Western Australia, is named.

Bunbury village, little changed in the forty or fifty years since this photograph was taken.

The Wild Boar, hotel and restaurant, is one of the most striking buildings in the district, what "Cheshire Country Houses" termed "an extravaganza in the Cheshire half-timbered style like a bad dream of Little Moreton Hall". It was formerly Beeston Towers, built in 1886 by the Naylor Brothers, John and Robert, who were successful timber merchants from Warrington. They were known far and wide from published accounts of their marathon walk, in 1871, from John O'Groats to Land's End.

John Naylor.

After the demise of the Naylors, Beeston Towers became a private boarding school for girls under the headship of the wonderfully-named Mrs Gabb. Later owners created a small restaurant and the Beeston Towers Country Club.

The property has been greatly altered and extended over the years, though upon close inspection a number of architectural quirks may be discerned, including two wood carvings of the Naylor brothers which depict how they saw each other.

Fittingly, Dr Barbara Moore who followed in the footsteps of the Naylors on the John O'Groats to Land's End walk, stayed here during her epic journey in 1960.

Robert Naylor.

Passing through Tarporley, 1960 – Dr Barbara Moore follows the feat of the Naylors.

The smithy in Beeston village, once part of the Peckforton estate. Records indicate that the blacksmiths at Beeston and nearby Tiverton worked on the building of Beeston Castle in the 13th century. The Clarke family were blacksmiths at Tiverton for two hundred years until the First World War. It is said that one of them was summoned to attend Eaton Hall, to shoe the Prince of Wales' (King Edward VII) horse and from that time onwards the Prince's Feathers were proudly displayed over the smithy door.

Pigs and carts in the middle of the Tarporley-Whitchurch road on busy days at Beeston Market at the turn of the 20th century! The Beeston Castle Hotel was formerly known as the Tollemache Arms.

The origins of Wright Manley's Beeston Castle Smithfield Market can be traced back to 1872, according to Brian Pennington in his splendid book "The Fall of the Hammer". The founder was Booth Hewitt, of The Rookery, Alpraham, who developed a string of livestock cattle markets adjoining railway stations, at Worleston, Calveley, Beeston, Tattenhall Road and Malpas. Though Malpas survived for a hundred years, Beeston alone warranted investment and continuation into the 21st century. Booth Hewitt's death occurred in 1896 following which the business was taken over by Joseph Wright. The lower photograph shows the opening, in 1975, of new offices (formerly the Royal Lancashire Showground's President's Pavilion) by television personality Ted Moult, with Alan and Harold Wright and Brian Pennington. (Reproduced courtesy of Brian Pennington)

ROAD, RAIL & CANAL

In the early years of the 20th century Beeston, on the main Crewe-Chester line, was one of the busiest country railway stations for miles around, not least because it served several main villages, the local farming community and the prosperous Beeston Cattle Market.

Services commenced in 1840 as part of the Grand Junction Railway with five intermediate stations between Crewe and Chester, at Worleston, Calveley, Beeston Castle & Tarporley, Tattenhall Road and Waverton. Today all these stations have closed; Tattenhall Road and Beeston were the last to go, in 1966. The Beeston Station buildings were demolished during the 1990s.

At one time, due to an agreement with Lord Tollemache, all passenger trains had to make a stop at Beeston and the efficient rail access encouraged many businessmen, particularly from the Merseyside area, to move to the countryside hereabouts.

Tilstone Lock and Tilstone Mill, probably in the 1920s.

Beeston Brook. A tranquil scene looking towards Tiverton from the railway bridge in the early 1900s. This was once a toll road with a gate at the top of Beeston Hill, removed in 1876. The road here crosses the canal, originally the Chester Canal, opened in 1772. Because of instability caused by numerous springs in the vicinity, the canal engineers had to use steel plates, rather than conventional bricks, to construct Beeston Lock.

Railway mania was at its height during this period and in 1905 plans were drawn up to build a light railway connecting Tarporley with the Chester-Manchester line at Mouldsworth. The scheme, promoted by Henry Haynes and Philip Crawshaw Hemingway, was approved by the Light Railway Commissioners with the cost of construction estimated at £46,000.

The 4ft-8 1/2in gauge line was mapped out from Tarporley along the A51 to Clotton, and near to Duddon Old Hall it veered off towards Prior's Heys and Kelsall Common, then crossed the main Chester highway and passed through Ashton to Mouldsworth Station. There were to be five bridges and two stations, one at Tarporley and the other near to Kelsall. Even the passenger fares were agreed: 3d per mile, first class; 2d per mile, second class; and 1d per mile third class. The approval allowed for five years to raise capital of £54,000 and to build the railway. Of course, it never came to fruition, presumably because the promoters were unable to sell 10,800 shares at £5 apiece.

Tattenhall had two stations. Tattenhall Road, alongside the Shropshire Union Canal, on the main Chester-Crewe line, and Tattenhall Junction, on the other side of the village, on the picturesque Whitchurch branch line, opened in 1872 and closed to passengers in 1957. Between Tattenhall and Whitchurch there were intermediate stations at Broxton and Malpas. This photograph is of "Station Road", towards Tattenhall Junction.

Beeston Station in its heyday. Only the station houses (right) remain.

Two local stations consigned to history. Above: Tattenhall Road (alongside the lane to Huxley) and Calveley, both on the main Chester-Crewe line. Similar to Beeston, there were cattle markets for many years alongside Tattenhall Road and Calveley stations.

Beeston Castle and Tarporley Station.

Awaiting the next train, outside Beeston Castle & Tarporley Station in the 1920s. The car parked under the canopy alongside the booking office suggests the arrival of one of the local bigwigs.

Beeston Station fell victim to Dr Beeching's axe in the 1960s.

From the rear of Beeston Station. Prior to the First World War a nine-hole golf course was located across the fields from Beeston Brook to Tilstone Bank and one of its keenest players was Lord Tollemache, of Peckforton Castle. In the 1890s Beeston Brook House was listed as a public house, appropriately named the "Railway and Canal Inn". This photograph, circa 1910, shows, on what is now the site of the Lock Gate Cafe, a group of early motorists apparently enjoying a picnic, complete with parasols.

Highwayside, Alpraham long ago. As the main route for Chester-London stage coaches, this was once Cheshire's principal road and from the 18th century there was a toll gate at Highwayside. Other toll gates in the immediate area were on Beeston Hill and near to Portal, on the outskirts of Tarporley. Turnpikes were universally unpopular and when the Beeston Hill gate ceased in 1876 one traveller wrote: "We shall all be rejoicing at having no longer to pull up in the midst of a steep hill to pay our tolls."

The two wide-beamed Bunbury Staircase Locks are a fascinating feature of the former Chester Canal which, since 1846, has been part of the Shropshire Union Canal system. Construction of the Chester Canal, under an Act of Parliament of 1772, opened up previously unthinkable trade to the villages of Calveley, Alpraham, Bunbury, Beeston, Tiverton and Tattenhall. The buildings seen to the right were stables for the canal horses.

TARPORLEY

Major restoration was carried out to the fabric of medieval St Helen's Church, Tarporley during the 1860/70s. The Tower which had been declared unsafe was completely rebuilt. The triangle formed by the Manor House, the Church and the Swan Hotel is thought to be the original village centre.

Swan Hotel and High St.

The Swan and the Market House, built by Sir John Crewe, early 18th century. Each morning the London-bound stagecoach (the "Royal Mail" during the 1830s) would call at 9.30 at the Swan Hotel, followed by the Birmingham-bound at 11.30. The return Chester coaches arrived each afternoon at 3.30.

Tarporley's earliest Police Station, in Park Road, (formerly Victoria Road), demolished in 1908.

High Street, with the Rising Sun public house to the left. Beyond, the trendy, "Chestnuts" shopping area has now replaced the white cottage and the other properties. The Rising Sun was kept for many years by the Woodward family until acquired by Robinson's Brewery. The shop was a saddlery.

Early 20th century scene of wheelwright's shop and cottages, Burton Square, at the end of Tarporley High Street. The left fork is Rode Street, towards Chester, and to the right is Utkinton Road. All these buildings have long since been demolished

The junction of Park Road and Cluetts Hotel (later the Perth Hotel).

Old Cottages, Tarporley.

Charming views of the old Clergy Houses which stood on High Street, opposite to the Old Fire Station.

In the days when cattle rather than cars blocked High Street, circa 1920, outside Cowap's Butcher's shop.

The Almshouses and the Bell & Lion public house. The Almshouses were erected in 1704 by Sir John Crewe for the use of poor widows. The plaque above the door has been retained and is mounted in the wall across the road from the present day National Westminster Bank. The Bell & Lion was trading as early as 1828 and survived until well into the 20th century.

Portal. Tarporley No. 5.

When these photographs were taken over seventy years ago no-one could possibly have envisaged that Portal would become a major golf centre. Until about 1860 the site of Portal was occupied by a modest, whitewashed farmhouse. This was purchased and developed by James Marshall Brooks, a Lancashire textile manufacturer, and inherited at the beginning of the 20th century by his nephew, the Hon. Marshall Brooks, Lord Crawshaw, who commissioned a new mansion, designed by W.E.Tower. During the First World War, Portal was one of several Red Cross hospitals in the district; others were housed in Bunbury Village Hall, Calveley Hall, Willington Hall and Peckforton Castle. The footbridge over Forest Road was built to link different parts of the Portal estate. The Portal golf development was launched in 1990 by the then owner, John Lilley.

The carriages and the early telegraph pole suggest this is a pre-1910 view of Tarporley High Street.

Salt's grocery shop, at the corner of High Street and Forest Road.

Edwardian perambulations in Tarporley.

This delightful view of High Street has changed little, except for the setts in front of the shops and the absence of cars! The one motor vehicle in sight is parked in front of the Old Fire Station.

These sandstone cottages, photographed sixty or seventy years ago, are still a feature of the Forest Road access into Tarporley village.

A little less traffic on Tarporley High Street during the 1950/60s.

TARPORLEY RACES

From the 1880s to the 1930s one of Cheshire's great sporting and social gatherings was Tarporley Hunt Races. On one day each year the village was literally turned on its head as thousands converged on the course in their carriages and carts, in their traps and on trains, on bicycle and on foot... a throng of humanity ready to gamble every last sixpence on the outcome of the Cheshire Farmers Cup or the Tarporley Handicap Chase.

Organised by the Hunt Club, the Tarporley Steeplechase meeting evolved from an original race staged at Crabtree Green, near Delamere, in 1766; seven members challenging each other for a sweep-

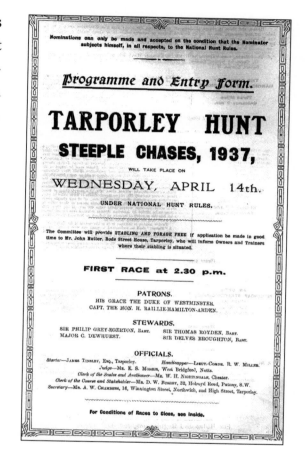

stake of 10 guineas each. In 1812, coinciding with the Act of Enclosure of Delamere Forest, the Tarporley meeting, by now an annual fixture in the official Racing Calendar, moved to a new course, with members' stand, alongside the Tarporley Road, at Cotebrook. This was part of Billington's Training Ground and Racecourse Lane, Sadlers Lane and Stand House survive to remind of those times.

Tarporley Races of 1890, from an engraving of an oil painting by Archibald MacKinnon.

Opening verses, Tarporley Races – 1862

One mornin' i' November, aw sed aw'd av a spree,
And aw'd goo an see the races on the coorse o' Tarporlee;
For aw thoght as workin' aw the day without a bit o' play
Wud make a chap grow seedy loik, an aw'd av a 'oliday !

So aw drew the plow besoides the doik and turn'd ow'd Farmer loose,
An weshed me feace and donned me best, and started for the coorse,
And there wot crowds o' folk aw seed as throng as honey bees,
Fro' scarlet coated noblemen to 'umbler folk i' frieze !

There wur drinkin' tents, and sta's wi nuts, an gingerbred, an pop,
Aunt Sally's mugs, an brass o'sticks – o' such a goodly crop;
There wer gipsy folk tow'd fortunes, an grooms as woise as they
Cud tell wich 'orse for sartin sure wud win the coop that day.

Aw seed sum four or foive o' these – a downy lot they looked
Who sed as 'ow the favourite was just as good as cooked;
One sed as Forester wos sure to carry off the proize,
For he'd been troid wi' racers loik, and when he goo's he flois.

Taking the last in the 1936 Tarporley Hunt Cup.

Racing at Cotebrook, traditionally on just a single Wednesday each April, came to an end in 1875 and for two years the Tarporley meeting was staged on fields behind the Swan Hotel. It then moved to Saighton, across the road from Saighton Grange, and finally returned to a permanent site in Tarporley, in 1877, something which met with a barrage of criticism from the editor (presumably the vicar) of the Tarporley Parish Magazine, of April 1878:

> Another course has been made at great expense of money and timber and the races are once more announced to be at Tarporley. How sorrowfully we regret this proposed interference with the quiet of our Lent, we cannot say; but still more do we regret the reintroduction amongst us of races which, though they may be for the harmless gratification of a few, are too often for the demoralisation of the many, if we may judge by the reports of the police, the complaints of the farmers and the sad story told by many homes, of the troubles caused by drink and betting.

The course was laid out on part of Lord Haddington's Arderne Estate, at Ash Hill, on the road to Chester, a mile from Tarporley village centre. It was circular,

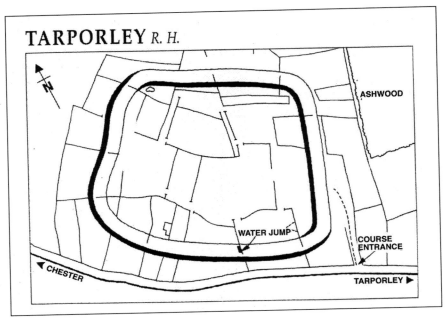

TARPORLEY R. H.

ASHWOOD

WATER JUMP

COURSE ENTRANCE

◄ CHESTER

TARPORLEY ►

Few walkers of the Sandstone Trail appreciate when they drop down from Fishers Green, past Ashwood to the A51 that they are passing alongside the former Tarporley Racecourse. The entrance was on the Tarporley side of the present day transport depot and the winning post was parallel with Ashwood.

right-handed, with a small railed parade ring, weighing room and paddock. Later additions included a public stand for 1,500 and a private stand for Hunt Club members and their guests and by the 1930s crowds could top 10,000, (8,000 in the two-bob cheap ring and the rest in the twelve shilling paddock enclosure).

Gordon Fergusson, in *Green Collars*, describes the course as having a long climb up to an exceptionally short run-in of 200 yards, often with tenacious going from the final fence. Tarporley was considered as a good a test as any for a true 'chaser' and many good horses and great horsemen did battle over the birch and gorse fences on the Cheshire grassland. The last ever race at Tarporley took place in April, 1939, a Novices' Steeplechase won by Benjamin Bunny, ridden by Mr Luke Lillington who, shortly afterwards, lost his life in wartime

France. Racing was cancelled for the duration of the Second World War and never revived at Tarporley despite strenuous efforts by members of the Hunt Club. The following are personal memories of Tarporley Races, penned in 1959 by Major Gilbert Cotton, a retired agent to Lord Tollemache (Peckforton Castle) and also Sir Philip Grey-Egerton (Oulton Hall):

> Before the advent of the motor-car Tarporley Races was an event of major importance in south Cheshire and vast numbers arrived by special trains at Beeston Castle and Cuddington stations from where it was possible to obtain transport to the racecourse, a matter of about three and a half miles, by horse-drawn vehicles at "a bob a nob". The 'transport' was drawn by a pair of rather weary looking horses which probably made several journeys during the morning. The roads for many miles present-ed a lively scene. There were four-in-hands, pairs and single horse vehi-cles. Often handfuls of coppers would be thrown into the road for the children who scrambled for them and villagers all turned out to see the fun when a coach horn was sounded to clear the road...

> Captain Billy Baldwin, who wore a beard, was a legendary character at Tarporley Races and on one occasion rode five winners in six races. He was a bachelor and lived at Cotebrook, when he was not hunting elephant or lion in Africa!

> Many celebrated horses won at Tarporley, but none was more popular than Mr Sam Challinor's Dreadnought who, in eight years, won the Farmers

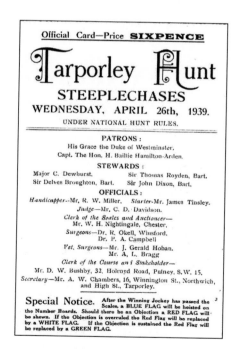

A programme from the last ever race meeting at Tarporley, in 1939.

"The Finish" ... Tarporley Races in 1898.

Race six times and was second twice. Mr Challinor used to drive him to the races in his 'shandy' and regularly took him to Beeston Market pulling a load of pigs or calves. Mr Arthur Brocklehurst and Mr Massey Harper were riding the only two runners in a steeplechase at Tarporley; they went slower and slower, eventually stopping on the far side where a very heated argument took place: they were great friends and also great rivals and it seems that one horse wouldn't jump without a lead and, of course, the other would not take the lead. They were on the point of coming to blows when the stewards sent word the race would be declared void unless it was completed in five minutes.

Detailed, and sometimes colourful accounts from Tarporley Races always appeared in the Chester Chronicle. One from the 1890s remarked upon "the splendid crowd, the aristocratic line of drags with much sipping of champagne, itinerant musicians, niggers, boxers, cripples and blacklegs, unflagging entertainment, a man with a coronet and irreproachable lung power, persistently singing The man that broke the bank of Monte Carlo."

The Tarporley and Beeston district has had a long and continuing association with horse racing, particularly the Grand National, and many famous thorough-breds made their names at Tarporley Races, or were trained hereabouts. Tipperary Tim, the astonishing 100-1 winner of the 1928 Grand National, won the Tarporley Open Chase and Gamecock, trained locally by Jimmie Jordan at Sandy Brow, registered a first triumph in the 1884 Foxhunters' Open. Three years later, and "specially trained" at Oulton Park, he won the Grand National. Another local winner was Grakle, in 1931, owned by C.R.Naylor, of Brook Hall, Tattenhall. In recent times, Amberleigh House, trained by Donald "Ginger" McCain, at Cholomondeley Castle, won the 2004 race, and in 2005 Carrie Ford rewrote racing history by finishing fifth on Forest Gunner, trained by her husband Richard, at Folly Farm, Oakmere.

LITTLE BUDWORTH, COTEBROOK & EATON

In the time of the Normans Little Budworth had a chapel held by St Mary's Benedictine Nunnery, Chester. It was known as the Free Chapel of Budworth-le-Frith. St Peter's Church, dating from the 16th century, was rebuilt in 1798-1800 and restored in 1870, by the leading Cheshire architect John Douglas.

This view, looking across Little Budworth Pool, has changed little since completion of the rebuilding of St Peter's Church in 1800.

The Village Tree, seen here about 1920, still stands at the centre of Little Budworth. Well Lane, to the left, is part of the ancient road from Tarporley to Over.

The Red Lion, Little Budworth, dates from the end of the 18th century and has been the favourite haunt for the past fifty years of numerous motor-sport stars visiting Oulton Park. One weekend guest for ever remembered was David Blakeley, a motor engineer and racing driver, who stayed here with his lover. She was Ruth Ellis, the last woman to be hanged in Britain. She died on the gallows in July 1955 after being found guilty of killing Blakeley.

Little Budworth may be the most charitable village in all England, thanks to three benefactors who lived in the 18th century. One gave parcels of land to the village, another left £1000 and a third bequeathed enough money to purchase a 157-acre farm to finance the building and upkeep of Little Budworth Almshouses which are still in use. The late Noel Parker (right) was Secretary of the Little Budworth Charities for 50 years.

The modes of transport seen here suggest that Little Budworth was just catching up with the 20th century... but only just!

Oulton Park Lodge, designed by Joseph Turner, of Whitchurch, and erected at a cost of £54 by William Eames during his landscaping of the park in 1775. The three arrows on the pinnacle of the building are from the Grey-Egerton coat of arms and denote the Egerton line.

Seventy years ago, looking from Brownhills, across the pool to Oulton Mill. The chimney alongside the mill suggests that by this time it was being driven by steam.

There was a working mill at Oulton for centuries, owned by the Egertons of Oulton and powered by Oulton Mill Pool. The last mill dated from 1781 and was abandoned around 1960. The earliest recorded name was Nogginshire Mill and the Cheshire Prophet, Robert Nixon, supposedly foretold that "three days' blood" would turn Nogginshire Mill and the "Lord of Oulton" would be hanged at his own door. In 1989 a fire gutted the building whilst it was being used as an antique and secondhand centre. A number of small streams flow into Oulton Pool, including one from a well at Rushton which, according to local legend, contained such healing properties that the sick, instantly cured of their ailments, left their crutches hanging in the trees! The Oulton Mill site has now been developed for housing. Nearby, off Forest Road, was Cotebrook Mill, the "Luddington Mill" of other Nixon prophesies. The Foden's Steam Wagon, photographed during the First World War, ran every working day during the 1920s, collecting grain from Liverpool for Oulton Mill.

St John's Church, Cotebrook (1874-75) was built at a cost of £1800, raised by public subscription. It was designed by G.E.Street and has a stained glass window by the Victorian Master of Glass, Charles Eamer Kempe. The lovely old white, thatched cottage, at one time the village bakehouse, was demolished in the late 1950s. The building to the right is Cotebrook C.E. School.

One for the archives. The stonemasons who built Cotebrook Church, the found ation stone of which was laid in 1873.

Cotebrook School, early 20th century, was the centre of village life until its closure in 1955. The building was demolished a few years later.

For hundreds of years the Alvanley Arms has been a popular watering-hole for travellers. In the 17th century it was a thatched coaching inn and as such serviced the south-bound stage coaches to and from Warrington. These possibly passed through Eaton village, rather than ascending Luddington Hill to Tarporley. Until the latter part of the 19th century, the Alvanley Arms was known as the Arden Arms. Cotebrook Smithy and the Smithy House stood at the far end of the car park, on the corner of Eaton Lane.

St John's Church and the Vicarage from Stable Lane. This view pre-dates the building of Cotebrook Village Hall in 1938.

Outside Cotebrook Post Office, in Harrop's Row, probably pre-First World War. Harrop's Row was just off Forest Road in Rushton Lane, now known as Oulton Mill Lane.

Harrop's Row cottages were demolished and the site acquired in the 1950s by Northwich Rural District Council.

The families of some of these children pictured sixty years ago, outside Forest Road cottages, probably still live in the area. The village post office was transferred from Harrop's Row to one of these cottages.

The hamlet of Cotebrook was called Utkinton-cum-Rushton until the opening of St John's Church in 1874/75. The modern name derives from a small brook, near to the Alvanley Arms, in which sheep were washed when "coted" or penned.

J.A.Holmes' Garage, Cotebrook. on the corner of Forest Road and Oulton Mill Lane. There was a farmhouse here and later Garner's Garage & Taxi Service. John Holmes acquired the business in 1937; it closed in 1987. During the days of the turnpikes, a toll cottage stood on the opposite Oulton Mill Lane corner.

Reflections of an age gone by – the bread cart on Fox Bank, Cotebrook.

The Water House, looking up Fox Bank, towards the Fox & Barrel.

The Fox & Barrel, Cotebrook, early 20th century. There may have been a crossroads here, with a lane from Over and Little Budworth cutting towards Kelsall. The Fox & Barrel supposedly got its name from a resourceful fox which took refuge in the pub cellar to escape the hounds. It is believed to have previously been titled the King's Head.

Little Budworth has been the centre of the Cheshire Polo Club since the 1930s. Here, circa 1960, Mrs M.Spiegelberg, presents the Amateur County Cup to HRH Prince Philip.

Quieter times on Jordan's Corner, the junction of the A54 and the A49, which takes its local name from Jimmie Jordan, the Sandy Brow-based racehorse trainer. The house Sandy Brow, parts of which date from the 17th century, was the Cheshire hunting residence of Colonel William Hall Walker (right), third son of Andrew Barclay Walker, an immensely rich brewer, who donated the Walker Art Gallery to the city of Liverpool. Colonel Hall Walker was a leading racehorse owner and breeder, and

founder of the National Stud, in 1916, when he sold to the nation his Tully Stud (Co. Kildare) and his stables in Wiltshire. He also gave all his bloodstock, initially for improving cavalry horses. In return he was created Baron Wavertree.

Eaton Cross at the turn of the 20th century. The absence of an early church seems to confirm there was a medieval preaching cross here. A new cross, to commemorate Queen Elizabeth's Silver Jubilee, was erected in 1977.

In 1886 a pipeline was laid to carry water from Lake Vyrnwy to Liverpool, passing through Beeston, Eaton and Cotebrook. A second pipeline was added forty years later. These are some of the workmen engaged on the later construction at Eaton. Shovels are still evident but steam had removed the hardest graft.

A smithy has stood at Eaton for centuries and remains a prominent feature of the village. The name "Eaton" is Anglo-Saxon and means a "settlement or village by water". Archaeological digs in 1980/81, on Eaton Cottage land, uncovered a section of Roman wall, part of a hypocaust and a medieval kiln. A cast of a giant footprint, found earlier at Eaton, is deposited in the British Museum, believed to be from a creature, dubbed "Chirotherium Herculis", of 230 million years ago.

There were eight farmhouses within a few hundred yards of Eaton Cross and a black-smith, farrier, wheelwright and saddler to serve them. Beyond the railings in this photo-graph is the doorway to a late Georgian building, old Eaton School, founded by Thomas Hough in 1806. The cottage, almost needless to say, was pulled down years ago.

The Wheelwright's workshop and cottage in Eaton, circa 1910, certainly seems to have been a place to meet and exchange village gossip. The workshop has gone, but the black and white cottage survives. It is the last dwelling on the right before leaving Eaton for Tiverton.

Eaton was once a village of charming thatched cottages. A few remain but most, including these here, succumbed to the planning vandals of the 20th century. The top photograph shows Ginny's Bank, now registered as common land, which is the last remnant of Eaton's ancient village green. Its name derives from the white, thatched cottage once occupied by one Ginny White. The lower photograph is of The Rock cottages, at the junction of Lightfoot Lane, shortly before their demolition in 1955.

THE FALL OF THE HOUSE OF GREY-EGERTON

It is difficult to imagine even the finest of fiction writers scripting the tragic story of Oulton Park, the ancestral home for almost five centuries of the Grey-Egertons. Queen Victoria was on the throne, Sir Philip Grey-Egerton was the 12th Baronet and the good folk of Little Budworth lined the lanes on christening day to welcome the arrival of twin sons, Rowland and Philp, an "heir and a spare". Everything was in its place, the lineage was assured and the homes and jobs of the villagers were safe for another generation.

Sir Philip Grey-Egerton's twin sons, Rowland and Philip who both lost their lives in the carnage of the First World War.

Sadly it was not to be; the distant drums of war saw to that. On August 14th, 1914 the First World War began and within twenty-two days of commencing active service Captain Rowland Grey-Egerton, of the 2nd Battalion Royal Welch Fusiliers, was dead, killed on the battlefields of Flanders. His brother, Philip, was more fortunate. For four long years he survived the carnage of the Western Front and with his health in tatters he returned to Oulton in 1918 to recuperate. His father, appreciating that the war was almost over, pleaded with him not to go back to France, but when the call came he insisted it was his duty to do so. Just days later he too was killed, in a mindless cavalry charge on an impregnable position during the Second Battle of Cambrai.

The outdoor staff and tenants at Oulton Park, circa 1912. The second, and rather eccentric, Lady Grey-Egerton kept the wallaby which roamed the grounds with two possums. Roy Ramsbottom's *Marching As To War* recounts the tale of her Ladyship presenting the trophies at a local cricket final, with a cockatoo perched on her shoulder.

The heart had gone out of Oulton and Sir Philip, devastated by the loss of his sons, leased the hall and parkland to a Mr Frank Cooper, Managing Director of the Partington Iron Works. It was whilst Mr Cooper was in residence, on St Valentine's Day 1926, that unimaginable tragedy struck again. Oulton Hall, the Grey-Egerton's stately pile, was ripped apart by a devastating fire and in attempting to salvage priceless works of art, six people lost their lives.

It was a Sunday morning, bright and clear, when a housemaid, up early to clean the grates, discovered the fire in her attic bedroom. Mr Cooper, settling down to breakfast with his family, immediately summoned Tarporley Fire Brigade which arrived within fifteen minutes. However it very quickly became apparent that their efforts were totally inadequate and the services of brigades from Chester, Winsford and Northwich were called out. By the time they reached the scene, Oulton Hall was an inferno and twenty estate workers and firemen were making a gallant effort to salvage paintings, furniture and personal effects. As they did so the roof timbers collapsed, bringing down a 30,000 gallon lead water tank. The head maid, Bertha Lloyd, an auxiliary maid, Mary Spann, and two young servants, Fred Crank and Harry White perished instantly. Later the

A local bobby keeps the crowd at a safe distance from the inferno.

Firemen from four brigades fought the blaze and flames could been seen for miles around. Hundreds turned up at the Oulton Park gates to witness the dreadful tragedy unfolding.

head gardener, George Sinclair, and a Tarporley fireman, Joseph Hunt, died in hospital as a result of terrible burns.

Major Gilbert Cotton, the Oulton agent, recalling the terrible scene said: "There were fifteen of us in the drawing room and the saloon, and some were mounted on ladders when someone shouted a warning. A huge crack was spotted in the ceiling and before any of us could make our escape the massive ceiling and rafters came crashing down. Flames and dense smoke enveloped us and the screams were terrible. Fortunately most of us escaped through some French windows. It was impossible for anyone to reach those trapped beneath the furnace."

So fierce was the fire that it wholly consumed the bodies of the four who died instantly and at the inquest, ten days later, the Coroner had to announce that because of insufficient evidence he would be unable to register the cause of the deaths, except in the case of Fireman Joseph Hunt which he recorded as accidental. Fireman Hunt was a bellringer at Tarporley Church and it is said that when called to the fire he was sounding the bells for morning service; he died from his injuries just as they were sounding for evening service. Sinclair, the head gardener, had only recently moved to Oulton from Peckforton Castle where he had held a similar position. Roy

The expanse of the great entrance hall with its high vaulted ceilings presented an impressive welcome to Oulton Hall.

Sir Philip Grey-Egerton examines the scene of devastation and lays a wreath for the six who perished in the Oulton Hall inferno.

A memorial service, conducted by the Bishop of Chester and six clergymen, was held on the charred terrace on the following Sunday.

Ramsbottom, *Marching As to War*, claims that great bitterness was felt amongst the families of the victims as they had not, in fact, "volunteered" to enter the house; they had been ordered to do so by Major Cotton.

On the Tuesday following the fire, Sir Philip, who had been holidaying in France with his second wife, arrived to see the grim scene for himself, "Dark Oulton", as he put it. The woman he had loved, his two sons and now his ancestral home had gone.

The cause of the fire was never established but it was generally thought to have been sparked by a fault in the electrical wiring in the roof space. Not everyone agreed and certainly some of the servants suspected a chimney fire. The damage was estimated at £250,000 and as the insurance, apparently, covered less than a third, it was not possible to rebuild Oulton Hall and for years it stood as a grim reminder of that awful St Valentine's Day of 1926.

Salvaging priceless works of art immediately after the fire. Many paintings were destroyed, including works by Van Dyck, Landseer, Romney and Lely. When the strongroom was opened a month later an entire day was required to tabulate the various items which included numerous racing trophies and the silver and plate from both the Cheshire Hunt and the Tarporley Hunt Club.

WAR AND PEACE

The charred remains of Oulton Hall stood as a monument to the lost years of the First World War. Many of the great families, not least the Grey-Egertons, had been decimated and by the outbreak of the Second World War, the old way, the aristocratic stranglehold that had dominated for centuries, was in terminal decline. It was, therefore, almost symbolic that Oulton Hall should be one of the early local casualties of the new conflict when a German bomber, returning from an aborted raid on Liverpool, dropped its deadly cargo on the ruins. Later the brick and stonework were carried away and the once tranquil Oulton Park settled down to a new chapter in its history, as a military camp, significantly as D-Day neared, for American troops. At one time or another Oulton also housed British, Canadian and Polish forces, as well as sailors of the French fleet, scuttled on the orders of Winston Churchill.

The original camp was built in 1939, although it was not until April 1940 that the required 159 acres were officially requisitioned. At that time the park was described as a "dismal shadow of its former glory". The first troops were British but in 1941 the site had to be enlarged to accommodate the Americans. The foundations of the camp roads were constructed from a double layer of used house bricks from blitzed sites in Liverpool.

Soon the "Yanks" began to arrive, to commence intensive training, most of them part of the American 3rd Army destined for the Invasion. Little Budworth Common was one of the earliest casualties, losing most of its trees to make way way for tank exercises for General Patton's troops. At Cholmondeley Castle there were thousands of Czechs and Poles who had escaped from Occupied Europe after Dunkirk. The Swan Hotel, Tarporley became the Battalion headquarters of the local Home Guard and Calveley Airfield, opened in March 1942 and planned as a fighter station, was a training centre for RAF pilots from Tern Hill and later

Until his death in 1937, Sir Philip Grey-Egerton and his wife took up residence in the grounds of Oulton Park. Here Lady Grey-Egerton, in an invalid chair, is with women from Little Budworth. A formidable character, she tried in vain to prevent the slaughter of the Oulton deer herd, on the orders of the War Agricultural Committee.

Shawbury. The drone of Harvards, Oxfords and Hurricanes was a familiar sound above the local countryside. At Sandy Brow, the extensive stables were used by Vickers Armstrong to store aeroplane parts and at Beeston, behind the cattle market, a fuel dump, away from the vulnerable ports and refineries, was established. For the most part the district escaped the worst ravages of the war although things did become decidedly fraught when a large number of incendiary bombs and landmines fell in the closing months of 1940. Bunbury Church was one of the buildings most severely damaged. The windows and half of one side were blown out and a row of nearby cottages totally destroyed. Elsewhere bombs rained down on Little Budworth Common, whilst at Cotebrook three farms were set alight and a house in Utkinton Lane was flattened.

The most bizarre experience was at Tirley Garth, as recounted by Irene Prestwich: "We women were all sent to sleep in the cellar. I hated it. I would rather have died in my bed. We could hear a terrific row as the planes passed overhead. That night thirty-six incendiary bombs fell in our garden. The next day was the 21st birthday of one of the girls who worked in the vegetable garden; and round her cake the bases of twenty-one incendiary bombs made excellent candlesticks!"

Another to recall these fraught times, specifically the night of November 28, 1940, was Little Budworth farmer Marcus Gilbert:

"The sirens sounded as usual about 8pm followed about 15 minutes later by the sound of the bombers. The whole area was illuminated by flares dropped from the first planes, then the whistle of bombs. The unforgettable sight of the whole area alight with the dazzling glare of hundreds of phosphorous incendiary bombs (about 15 inches long and two inches in diameter). These bombs easily penetrated the roofs of buildings and it was not long before several caught fire. Then there was a lull in the bombing. Pitch black everywhere. Chaotic! Vehicles colliding, a huge crater in the middle of the A49, surrounded by a four-foot wall of sand, into which a motor lorry, loaded with Christmas trees, had come to rest, with its bonnet over the edge of the crater. A broken main pipe was filling the crater with water. The second wave of bombers and now it was panic, everyone diving for cover. The big tap room table in the Cabbage Hall was considered to be a relatively safe haven (if you could manage to get under it). The Egerton Arms was also a place of refuge. Sandy Brow and the Cabbage Hall."

Bombed and badly damaged, Bunbury Church was not fully restored until the 1950s.

Cotebrook was one of many platoons in the district, part of the 14th Battalion Cheshire Home Guard.

Meanwhile, like Oulton Park, Tarporley Racecourse was also being commandeered in 1940, for the construction of an army camp, with barracks for about 800 men, principally from the Royal Artillery and the Royal Signals. Later, from the end of 1941, Tarporley Camp housed German and Italian prisoners, many of whom worked on local farms. After the war, and until the 1960s, there was a Royal Observer Corps' post here, engaged in spotting aircraft in the event of nuclear attack. In preparation for such an emergency, underground bunkers and a giant storage depot, for essential food and emergency equipment, were installed in the 1950s.

One unit stationed at Oulton Park during the war was the US 232nd Station Hospital, out of Camp Maxey, Texas. Following an Atlantic crossing on board the Mauritania and a rail journey, "twenty five miles southwest to the small station of Beeston", the unit commander noted the damp and cold at Oulton, a "big contrast from the warmth of Texas". Many of the men and nurses were affected by respiratory illness during the first month as the "Cheshire rain drizzled down day after day".

The entire campsite was a sea of mud and the 232nd set about building boardwalks, improving roads and drainage and generally making their new home into something more habitable. "We had trained as Medics," he complained, "but we worked as engineers. We could have built roads right across England if we had been given the time!"

Towards the end of the war many American units arrived en route for the final push into Germany. One was the 90th Chemical Mortar Battalion (Fort Bragg) which left Oulton and fought its way to the Remagen Bridgehead and on to the Danube river at the close of hostilities. Lt. Col. Edgar V.H.Bell, commanding officer, kept a diary of the Battalion's stay at Oulton, in "Nissen huts, cold and drafty, with bunks made from jeep packing cases adorned with straw ticks, came to us through lease lend":

"January 5th, 1945: Sumptuous dinner, chicken and FF potatoes, good and hot. Ours is a wonderful mess crew. Told Taylor to go to London to find out about his transfer. He is no good to us. Mopes and cries in his beard all the time. Wants no part of combat.

January 16th: The General Court sat here today. We acquitted a kid accused of rape at Tarporley. I broke the case to hell with one question. The kid cried all over me. Slapped a lieutenant with dismissal and two years hard labour. He borrowd $2,175 from 6 EM in two months. The son-of-a-bitch.

January 18th: Some soldier slugged a taxi driver, took his money and cab last night. All personnel restricted to camp.

January 28th: Up at 0300 to breakfast to see ADV party off. Washed clothes and packed gear. To Tattenhall for supper.

January 31st: Hit Camp C-1 at Southampton. Horrible filthy hole. Tore a British sergeant's ass out for cursing my men. Then tore a British major for letting his sergeant do it. Both vanished into the night. Got the men under cover and fed. Took over British officers' club by brute force."

Lt. Col. Bell concluded his diary entries on Oulton with the following: "A liberal pass was inaugurated permitting men to visit the famous cities of London,

Liverpool and Manchester. Even the historic Roman walls of Chester afforded a certain fascination for those who favoured English femininity. All will remember such places as Clemences, Shrewsbury Arms, Green Dragon, White Swan, and the burning Scotch and cheap gin, warm beer and tasteless food."

As well as attracting military personnel, the Tarporley and Beeston district's relative safety was a haven for evacuees from some of the major cities and throughout the war there were almost as many 'displaced' children as there were

An aerial view of Tarporley Racecourse camp at Ash Hill in 1947. The Chester Road and Ashwood are clearly visible, as are the footprints of some of the racecourse structures.

troops. A classic account of these times was penned years later by Lady Marjorie Bibby, the wife of Sir Charles Bibby, of Tilstone Lodge:

"We were to take evacuee children from Liverpool; we had been allotted twenty-five. I managed to persuade the billeting officer that stable loose boxes were not suitable for children in mid-winter, and was finally told to take fifteen. Luckily a ship was being converted in Birkenhead, so I was able to get bedding, crockery and cutlery, in fact everything except beds. The children slept on mattresses on the floor for two nights and then I got camp beds. The great day arrived and I went down to the local school where 300 children from Holy Trinity School, Wavertree had arrived in buses. My quota were aged between five and fifteen, boys and girls including three pure Chinese. I went down to the station to tell the senior billeting officer we were ok and found him sitting surrounded by six young mothers with infants who had come by mistake. I packed them in the car and took them home.

"The last tired infant was just going to sleep when a stentorian bellow came from the front hall where stood my mother, having motored from Aberdeen en route for Hampshire with three of her staff. She planned to spend the night at the Swan Hotel but found it full of Army. Anyhow we managed to get them all in. I think we were 32 sleeping in the house that night! The vacs went to the local school and got their dinners there, a tremendous help with the rations. I went to Marks & Spencers in Chester and fitted them all out, head to toe. I put the children's own clothes into bags with their names on and took them to the laundry (we had our own in those days). My laundress drew herself up and said 'I wouldn't touch them with a barge pole, they're 'ummin'. And that was the end of my laundry.

"We were on on the edge of the gun barrage

A letter from Cologne in 1946, to a German soldier in 74 P.O.W. camp, Tarporley.

protecting Liverpool Docks and the marshalling yards at Crewe, so had warning sirens practically every night. We decided to convert the cellar and every night for eighteen months the children, grasping their potties, went safely to bed and our own youngsters slept in the boiler house. On the second anniversary of the vacs' arrival we had a magnificent crater made by a bomb in an adjacent field, and celebrated with a picnic in the hole. I was air-raid warden for our little area and was supposed to have been issued with a tin hat, but never got one, so on noisy nights I wore an aluminium saucepan on my head, with the handle down my back. My husband went into Liverpool by train each day, as although some of the ships were taken over by the Royal Navy he had to staff and manage the hospital and troopships. In the evenings he trained the Home Guard.

"We were very lucky as one night there was a big raid and a lot of incendiary bombs were dropped, one missed the nursery window by about a foot. We were lit up like a circus arena and with the constant throb of raiders passing overhead. We had bug-hunting sessions every night, with towels round our shoulders and a fine comb dipped in Dettol, and seldom missed a find. Our son John's war was ruined as he was the only one who never had a little visitor!

"The vacs were of course city dwellers so I tried to teach them a little countrylore, about ducks and drakes, sheep and rams, acorns on oak trees, conkers and chestnut trees. There was only one girl who stayed the whole five years; as they got older their parents wanted them home to earn some money. The children certainly benefited from the good food and country air and, I think and hope, from the care and affection they received."

After 1945 life slowly returned to normal as the great clear-up commenced, across the entire area, of the military occupation. Nowhere were the scars more acutely evident than at Oulton Park where hundreds of huts lay derelict amidst concrete bases, water towers and a criss-cross of tarmacadam; a far cry, indeed, from the once magnificent parkland. The final chapter in Oulton's long and illustrious history had apparently been written and with the 14th Baronet Grey-

Reggie Tongue drops the flag to start the historic Formula 500 heat, the first ever race at Oulton Park, on August 8, 1953. The winner Don Truman is at the front of the grid, extreme left.

Egerton seeking due compensation from the Government, there seemed every likelihood that the site would be sold.

Fortunately a small group of motor racing enthusiasts, led by Ray Dawson and Eric Grimsditch of the Mid Cheshire Motor Club, had other ideas and in due course the site was leased from the Grey-Egertons. A motor-racing circuit was very quickly created from the old camp roads and on August 8th, 1953 the famous pre-war racing driver Reggie Tongue, the new President of the Mid Cheshire Motor Club, dropped the flag to start Oulton Park's first ever race, a Formula 500 heat which, for the record, was won by Don Truman. This was a private trial to test the suitability of the circuit and when the inaugural public meeting took place, on October 3rd, more than 40,000 were in attendance. Over the ensuing fifty-plus years Oulton Park has attracted many of the greatest names in motor sport and is still considered to be one of the foremost circuits in Britain.